777

Quotes
to
Rule Your Life

READ THE QUOTES FROM YESTERDAY, TODAY, TO CONQUER TOMORROW

Gianni Grassotti

BookLeaf Publishing

Presentation by *BookLeaf Publishing*

Web: www.bookleafpub.com

E-mail: info@bookleafpub.com

ISBN: 9789363301122

First edition 2024

To my parents:

"I am forever grateful for the ones who taught me how to be not just a man but a gentleman."

Rule #1:

“Take care of the home before impressing the streets.”

-Vito Corleone (The Godfather 1972 Film)

Rule #2:

“Money might make you rich, but respect and politeness make you a gentleman.”

-Fabio Attanasio

Rule #3:

“Never let success get to your head; never let failure get to your heart.”

-Ziad K. Abdelnour

Rule #4:

“If you want to own a Rolls-Royce, stop taking advice from a Toyota owner.”

-Warren Buffet

Rule #5:

“Give a man a gun, and he will rob a bank. Give a man a bank, and he will rob the world.”

-Salvatore (Lucky) Luciano

Rule #6:

“To succeed greatly, you must be able to fail greatly.”

-Mike Tyson

Rule #7:

“Every journey begins with a single step. We just have to have patience.”

-Milly Thompson

Rule #8:

“The sky is not my limit; I am.”

-T.F Hodge

Rule #9:

"There is no passion in playing small - in settling for a life that is less than the one you are capable of living."

-Nelson Mandela

Rule #10:

"It's not the length of a life but the depth."

-Ralph Waldo Emerson

Rulc #11:

"A man can make money, but money can never make a man."

-Anonymous

Rule #12:

"If you don't like your destiny, don't accept it."

-Naruto Uzumaki

Rule #13:

"If betrayal and loyalty meant nothing then the devil would still be sitting next to God"

-Gianni Grassotti

Rule #14:

"It is just pathetic to give up on something before you give it a shot."

-Reiko Mikami

Rule #15:

"Impossible. A word to be found only in the dictionary of fools."

-Napoleon Bonaparte

Rule #16:

"They say making money is hard. I say making money is an art."

-Anonymous

Rule #17:

“The impossible only becomes possible for the ones who tried even when all the odds were against them.”

-Gianni Grassotti

Rule #18:

“Do it alone, Do it broke, Do it tired, Do it scared. Just do it.”

-Meryl Streep

Rule #19:

“A man is not great because he has not failed; a man is great because failure has not stopped him.”

-Confucius

Rulc #20:

"Winners will always find a way. But losers will always find an excuse."

-Anonymous

Rule #21:

"All things are possible for the one who believes"

-Mark 9:23

Rule #22:

"Courage does not mean you don't get afraid. Courage means you don't let fear stop you."

- Bethany Hamilton

Rule #23:

"For many are called. But few are chosen."

-Matthew 22:14

Rule #24:

"Men in suits look successful until you realize they work for men in jeans."

-Anonymous

Rule #25:

"There is nothing impossible to him who will try."

-Alexander the Great

Rule #26:

"Don't complain about what you didn't get from work; you didn't put in."

-Anonymous

Rule #27:

"Don't let someone who gave up on their vision talk you out of yours."

-Salvatore (Sally Slices) Mandreucci

Rule #28:

"You are one step away from everybody acting like they saw the vision from the start."

-Anonymous

Rule #29:

"Failure is simply the opportunity to begin again, this time more intelligently."

-Henry Ford

Rule #30:

"Once you reach the peak, you will realize it isn't a mountain you conquered but yourself."

-Anonymous

Rule #31:

"Work hard and become a leader; be lazy and become a slave."

-Proverbs 12:24

Rule #32:

"YOU CAN EITHER KEEP GRINDING OR GIVE UP. They are both going to hurt."

-Anonymous

Rule #33:

"I want you to fail, then I want you to get up and do it again."

-Tom Platz

Rule #34:

"You are living at least one of the prayers you used to pray."

-Chelsea Miles

Rule #35:

"For God will steer the boat, but you need to row. God will give you the tools to succeed, but you must apply them to win."

-Gianni Grassotti

Rule #36:

"At the end of the game, the king and the pawn go back into the same box."

-Anonymous

Rule #37:

"The further society drifts from the truth, the more it will hate those who speak it."

-George Orwell

Rule #38:

"Believe in yourself because if you don't, no one will."

-Marilyn Monroe

Rule #39:

"Nowadays, people know the price of everything, but the value of nothing."

-Oscar Wilde

Rule #40:

"The biggest wall you need to climb is the one in your mind."

-Anonymous

Rule #41:

"Slow success builds character; fast success builds ego. Don't pray for quick success; pray to have the wisdom to make it stick."

-Iman Gadzhi

Rule #42:

"When money speaks, no one checks the grammar."

-Anonymous

Rule #43:

"When I fall, I shall arise; when I sit in darkness, the Lord shall be a light unto me."

-Micah 7:8

Rule #44:

"A winner is just a loser who never gave up."

-Dana White

Rule #45:

"Good judgment comes from experience, and Experience comes from poor judgment."

-Frank Sinatra

Rule #46:

"People will come back into your life after being disappointed by the people they thought were better than you."

-Anonymous

Rule #47:

"To have confidence that no one can break, you have to be able to walk into a room like God sent you there."

-Gianni Grassotti

Rule #48:

"The two most important days in your life are the day you are born, and the day you realize why you were born."

-Branden Holder

Rule #49:

"If you ask God for help and hear nothing, remember teachers are silent during tests."

-Sage Kenny

Rule #50:

"First, they call you crazy, then they hate on you. Then they ask you how you did it, and finally, ask you for a job."

-Codie Sanchez

Rule #51:

"You wouldn't have a Dream or desire unless it were in your power to make it true."

-Anonymous

Rule #52:

"Bees don't waste their time explaining to flies that honey is better than crap."

-TeeJay Britton

Rule #53:

"It is hard to stay faithful when you are winning."

-Future

Rule #54:

"If a friend gets into a fight, join it no matter how strong they are."

-Anonymous

Rule #55:

"Losers let it happen; winners make it happen."

-Denis Waitley

Rule #56:

"Don't stop when you're tired. Stop when you're done."

-David Goggins

Rule #57:

“By pushing through and going that one more round, you discovered what life is all about.”

-Sylvester Stallone

(Rock lV, 1985 film)

Rule #58:

“If you are good at something, never do it for free.”

-Heath Ledger

Rule #59:

"If you are going through hell, keep on going."

-Winston Churchill

Rule #60:

"Some people are bills, and some people are investments."

-Marques Prince

Rule #61:

"A lawyer and his briefcase can steal more than ten guys with guns."

-Al Capone

Rule #62:

"When it feels scary to jump in, that is exactly when you jump in. Otherwise, you will always be in the same place your whole life."

-Oscar Issac

Rule #63:

"Strong enough to have it all, too weak to take it."

-Green Goblin

(Amazing Spider-Man 2012 Film)

Rule #64:

"Defeat is a state of mind; no one has been defeated until defeat has been accepted as a reality."

-Anonymous

Rule #65:

"For a man to conquer himself is the first and noblest of all victories."

-Plato

Rule #66:

"A rock in bad hands killed Abel. A rock in good hands killed Goliath."

-Anonymous

Rule #67:

"It's easy not to care what others think about you when you don't think about them."

-Gianni Grassotti

Rule #68:

"The Devil wouldn't keep attacking if you didn't have something valuable inside you. Just like how thieves don't break into empty houses."

-Anonymous

Rule #69:

"Get your mind out of the gutter and get in the gym."

-Gianni Grassotti

Rule #70:

"A weak man will be abused. A nice man will be used. A ruthless man will be feared. A true man will be respected."

-Ashley Cox

Rule #71:

"If the freedom of speech is taken away, then dumb and silent we may be lead like sheep to the slaughter."

-George Washington

Rule #72:

"When a man hunts, he does not chase after a deer. He will let it run and patiently wait for another one."

-Anonymous

Rule #73:

"When tyranny becomes law, rebellion becomes duty."

-Thomas Jefferson

Rule #74:

"Revenge has no expiry date. I'll be back when I'm ready."

-Anonymous

Rule #75:

"Can cowards tell you to have courage

Can Atheists say Help me, God

Can narcissists say I love you

Well then, can dictators say freedom."

- Andrew Tate

Rule #76:

"Boys sacrifice their future; men sacrifice their present."

-Shuja

Rule #77:

"Be like glass; if they break you, cut them."

-Bruce Lee

Rule #78;

"If only size mattered, then the elephant would be the king of the jungle."

-Oleksandr Usyk

Rule #79:

"Every day above ground is a good day."

-Mel Bernstein

(Scarface, 1983 Film)

Rule #80:

"Dream as if you will live forever; live as if you will die today."

-James Dean

Rule #81:

"Choose a friend that is better than you."

-Steven Crea

Rule #82:

"Fear no man on this earth. For you should be a mighty lion among wild beasts."

-Anonymous

Rule #83:

"I'm not saying I am the best at what I do; I'm just saying it's me against whoever wants to lose."

-Drake

Rule #84:

"If you think the price of winning is too high, just wait until you get the bill from regret."

-K.J.B

Rule #85:

"I trained four years to run for 9 seconds, and people give up when they don't see results in 2 months."

-Usain Bolt

Rule #86:

"To get something you never had, you must do something you have never done."

-Simon Daood

Rule #87:

"The secret to success is to do the common things uncommonly well."

-John Rockefeller

Rule #88:

"The people that criticized you for trying to be exceptional are those who have already accepted that they will be mediocre for the rest of their lives."

-Stephen Castro

Rule #89:

"If you have no confidence in yourself, you are defeated twice in the race of life. If you have confidence, you won before the race started."

-Cicero

Rule #90:

"Ignore a boy, and he will chase you. Ignore a man, and he will replace you."

-Anonymous

Rule #91:

"Don't chase after women and lose your strength; women like that have destroyed kings."

-Proverbs 31:3

Rule #92:

"The clever are not so much looking for loneliness, as they avoid the fuss created by fools."

-Arthur Schopenhauer

Rule #93:

"Boys with no self-control become men behind bars."

-Kwame Alexander

Rule #94:

"A boy knows what he wants and waits for someone to help him. A man knows what he wants and gets it done."

-Anonymous

Rule #95:

"My Grandparents came here with nothing and made something. Not for me to have something and do nothing."

-Gianni Grassotti

Rule #96:

"Non-Perdis operam"

(Don't waste your time)

-Anonymous

Rule #97:

"A daughter will have the same qualities as their mother, just like a son will have the same morals as their father. So choose wisely."

-Pietro Grassotti

Rule #98:

"Forgive your enemies, but never forget their names."

-John F. Kennedy

Rule #99:

"Keep your friends close, but your enemies closer."

-Al Pacino

(Godfather 1972 Film)

Rule #100:

"Three things never come back. Time, Word, and opportunity."

-Confucius

Rule #101:

"Never sit at a table where they talk about others because you're the next topic when you get up."

-Tupac Shakur

Rule #102:

"Let people talk behind your back. They're behind you for a reason."

-Rey Faja

Rule #103:

"You have enemies? Good, that means you stood up for something. Sometime in your life"

-Winston Churchill

Rule #104:

"My enemies are many, my equals are none"

-Napoleon Bonaparte

Rule #105:

"Only a fool trips over what lies behind him"

-Anonymous

Rule #106:

"The LORD hears his people when they call to him for help. He rescues them from all their troubles".

-Psalms 34:17

Rule #107:

"You will suffer for a short time. But after that, God will make everything right".

-1Peter 5:10

Rule #108:

"Go ahead and be angry. You do well to be angry. But don't use your anger as fuel for revenge".

-Ephesians 4:26-27

Rule #109:

"Two traps you need to avoid. One is caring what they think. Two is thinking they care."

-Gathee Wa Njeri

Rule #110:

"It is more damaging for a minister to say foolish things than to do them."

-Cardinal de Retz

Rule #111:

"Birds can't teach fish how to swim, so why are women trying to teach men how to be men?"

-Anonymous

Rule #112:

"And he shall bring their iniquity upon them and cut them off in their wickedness."

-Psalm 94:23

Rule #113:

"Don't tell everyone your dreams. New dreams attract new enemies and haters. Work in silence and let God do what he wants to do in your life, let God surprise your enemies."

-Anonymous

Rule #114:

"Winning doesn't make you heartless. But it teaches you to use your heartless."

-Tim Grover

Rule #115:

"If the plan doesn't work, then change it. Never the goal."

-Anonymous

Rule #116:

"If you only do what you can do, you will never be more than you are."

-Master Shifu

(Kung Fu Panda, 2008 film)

Rule #117:

"If it weren't hard, everyone would do it. It's the hard that makes it great."

-Tom Hanks

Rule #118:

"If you do as you have always done, you will get what you have always gotten."

-Tony Robbins

Rule #119:

"Focusing on goals instead of focusing on girls is the best decision a young man can make."

-Anonymous

Rule #120:

"You will face men who love death as much as you love life."

-Khalid ibn Al-Walid

Rule #121:

"A man should not train to be a bodybuilder, He should train to be a weapon in all aspects of his life."

-Gianni Grassotti

Rule #122:

"He who sweats more during training will bleed less during the war."

-Spartans

Rule #123:

"Insanity is doing the same thing, over and over again, but expecting different results."

-Albert Einstein

Rule #124:

"The best revenge is massive success."

-Frank Sinatra

Rule #125:

"You learn a lot about people when they don't get what they want from you."

-Richard Cooper

Rule #126:

"A man who has the strength to pray for his enemies has the power to defeat them without lifting a finger."

-Gianni Grassotti

Rule #127:

"What if God ruined your plans so that your plans wouldn't ruin you?"

-Proverbs

Rule #128:

"When the time is right, I, the Lord, will make it happen."

-Isaiah 60:22

Rule #129:

"There is no other option than to stay loyal, kind, caring, and helpful. God is watching, karma is waiting, and the devil is plotting."

-Anonymous

Rule #130:

"In school, you learn things, and then you are given the test; with God, you are given the test, and then you learn things."

-Andrew Tate

Rule #131:

"If you don't stand for something, you will fall for anything."

-Peter Marshall

Rule #132:

"Educating the mind without educating the heart is no education at all."

-Aristotle

Rule #133:

"You can't win the war against the world if you have not won the battle with your mind."

-Anonymous

Rule #134:

"Never argue. In society, nothing must be discussed; give only results."

-Benjamin Disraeli

Rule #135:

"Patience is when you're supposed to get mad but choose to understand."

-Anonymous

Rule #136:

"Let your plans be dark and impenetrable as night. And when you move, fall like a thunderbolt."

-Sun Tzu

Rule #137:

"Do not compare yourself to others; if you do so, you insult yourself as no two people are the same."

-Karen DiSanto

Rule #138:

"To make anyone immediately regret insulting you. Show that you are unaffected."

-Miyamoto Musashi

Rule #139:

"The only time you should look back is to see how far you have come."

-Anonymous

Rule #140:

"For God has not given us a spirit of fear and timidity but of power, love, and self-discipline."

-2 Timothy 1:7

Rule #141:

"Success doesn't come from those who wish for it; it comes from those who work for it consistently even when they don't feel like it."

-Anonymous

Rule #142:

"If God is for us, who can be against us?"

-Romans 8:31

Rule #143:

"If you avoid conflict to keep the peace, you start a war inside yourself."

-Cheryl Richardson

Rule #144:

"Behold, I give unto you the power to tread on serpents and scorpions, and over all the power of the enemy: and nothing shall by any means hurt you."

-Luke 10:19

Rule #145:

"Even if a man loses everything, He still has God and himself. That's enough to start all over again."

-Roshan Lamichhane

Rule #146:

"For a just man falleth seven times, and riseth up again: but the wicked shall fall into mischief."

-Proverbs 24:16

Rule #147:

"At your lowest, you will see the real faces of people."

-Dana Grassotti

Rule #148:

"If you are lonely alone, you are in bad company."

-Jean-Paul Sartre

Rule #149:

"Don't let the bad days make you think you have a bad life."

-Johnny Depp

Rule #150:

"Keep working until you don't have to introduce yourself."

-Salvatore (Sally Slices) Mandreucci

Rule #151:

"To dream of millions is by myself, to dream of billions is by my brothers."

-Gianni Grassotti

Rule #152:

"Don't let someone kill your dreams just because they already killed theirs."

-Salvatore (Sally Slices) Mandreucci

Rule #153:

"Fear has killed more dreams than failure ever will"

-Jatinder Singh

Rule #154:

"The moment you realize your success is when you should pray to God and thank him, for without God, you have nothing."

-Gianni Grassotti

Rule #155:

"When you get what you want, that's God's direction. When you don't get what you want, that's God's protection."

-Psalms

Rule #156:

"The problem with the world is that the intelligent people are full of doubts, while the stupid ones are full of confidence."

-Charles Bukowski

Rule #157:

"Behind every great man is a woman who pushed him to his limits."

-Mark Twain

Rule #158:

"Don't lose your mind over someone who doesn't mind losing you."

-Salvatore (Sally Slices) Mandreucci

Rule #159:

"Your opinion has never paid my bills."

-Nikita Valdimirov

Rule #160:

"Neutral men are the devils, Allie's."

-Salvatore (Lucky) Luciano

Rule #161:

"A wise man learns more from his enemies than a fool from his friends."

-Baltasar Gracian

Rule #162:

"You can judge a man by the power of his enemies"

-Andrew Tate

Rule #163:

"Never let your pride get in the way. Being able to do what is necessary to provide for your family."

-Anonymous

Rule #164:

"It is easier to find men who will volunteer to die than to find those who are willing to endure pain with patience."

-Julius Caesar

Rule #165:

"A man who can not control himself will never truly be free."

-Gianni Grassotti

Rule #166:

"Never interrupt your enemy when he is making a mistake."

-Napoleon Bonaparte

Rule #167:

"The lion is not the strongest, biggest, or fastest animal but the wisest. That is why the lion is the king."

-Ray Lewis

Rule #168:

"He who fears being conquered is sure to be defeated."

-Napoleon Bonaparte

Rule #169:

"Most people don't want the truth. They want the constant reassurance that what they believe in is the truth."

-Friedrich Nietzsche

Rule #170:

"If it's the right person, it's never the wrong time."

-Salvatore (Sally Slices) Mandreucci

Rule #171:

"If you wouldn't get a car with a nice exterior but an ugly interior, why would you go for the same setup in a person?"

-Anonymous

Rule #172:

"A man is not defined by the amount of money he's made in his life, but by the impact he has made on the world around him."

-Bob Marley

Rule #173:

"Nothing truly stops you. Nothing truly holds you back. For your own will is always within your control."

-Epictetus

Rule #174:

"A true soldier fights not because he hates what's in front of him but because he loves what's behind him."

-G.K Chesterton

Rule #175:

"Whoever said the pen is mightier than the sword never encountered automatic weapons."

-General McAuther

Rule #176:

"If you let a person talk long enough, you will hear their true intentions."

-Tupac Shakur

Rule #177:

"You must break out of your comfort zone if you ever want to break the generational standards."

-Gianni Grassotti

Rule #178:

"Confidence is loud, and insecurities are louder."

-Steve Magness

Rule #179:

"There is no dishonor in losing the race. There is only Dishonor in not racing because you are afraid to lose."

-Gareth Stein

Rule #180:

"Dreams mean nothing if you leave them on your pillow."

-Anonymous

Rule #181:

"The man who asks questions is a fool for a minute; the man who does not ask is a fool for life."

-Confucius

Rule #182:

"The outcome of a young man's conversations should be income."

-Gianni Grassotti

Rule #183:

"There's always going to be someone who disagrees with what you say."

-Andrew Tate

Rule #184:

"God allowed them to walk away because you prayed for a good person, and they were not."

-Anonymous

Rule #185:

"Devote the rest of your life to making progress."

-Epictetus

Rule #186:

"Everyone must choose one of two paths. The pain of discipline or the pain of regret."

-Jesse Randell

Rule #187:

"You are what you do, not what you'll say you will do."

-Carl Jung

Rule #188:

"When a boy is heartbroken he finds another girl. When a man is heartbroken, he finds himself"

-Anonymous

Rule #189:

“A conqueror is always a lover of peace.”

-Carl Von Clausewitz

Rule #190:

“Vincere aut mori”

(conquer or die)

-Anonymous

Rule #191:

“I always say you should aim for peace. But if you can’t aim for peace, aim between the eyes.”

-Conor McGregor

Rule #192:

“A season of loneliness and isolation is when a caterpillar gets its wings.”

-Mandy Hale

Rule #193:

“Better to fight for something than to live for nothing.”

-George S. Patton

Rule #194:

"The best way to stay hungry is to hang out with winners. They push each other to accomplish more."

-Gianni Grassotti

Rule #195:

"He who cannot live in society must be either a beast or a God."

-Aristotle

Rule #196:

"Don't be mad at the clown when you keep going to the circus."

-Anonymous

Rule #197:

"Lack of activity destroys the good condition of every human being."

-Plato

Rule #198:

"Failed with God,

Cried with God,

Suffered with God,

Succeeded with God"

-Lesane Homie

Rule #199:

"I would rather stand by God and be condemned by the world than stand by the world and be condemned by God."

-Denzel Washington

Rule #200:

"Be happy with what you got while working for what you want."

-Hellen Keller

Rule #201:

"Not everyone who offers a hand is trying to lift you; some people are just trying to drag you down."

-Gianni Grassotti

Rule #202:

"Never become so hungry that you eat from any plate presented to you."

-Dan Martell

Rule #203:

"To break the rules, you must first master them."

-Audemars Piguet

Rule #204:

"Be careful. The devil can hear your prayers, too; he doesn't always come dressed with a pitchfork and horns. Sometimes, he can come dressed as everything you ever wanted."

-Anonymous

Rule #205:

"For what shall it profit a man if he shall gain the whole world and lose his soul?"

-Mark 8:36

Rule #206:

"Don't expect people to understand your grind when God didn't give them your vision."

-Tony Gaskins Jr.

Rule #207:

“Sometimes people don’t want to hear the truth because they don’t want their illusions destroyed.”

-Fredrick Nietzsche

Rule #208:

“It is not the actual physical exertion that counts towards a man’s progress. But the spirit of faith with which is undertaken”.

-St Francis Xavier

Rule #209:

“There are four steps for a happy life. Get rid of anyone who 1) Lies to you, 2) Disrespects you, 3) Uses you, 4) Puts you down”

-Frank Sinatra

Rule #210:

“Forget what hurt you, but don’t forget what it taught you.”

-Hiro Mashima

Rule #211:

“You will never find the right one. If you never let go of the wrong one.”

-Salvatore (Sally Slices) Mandreucci

Rule #212:

"The comeback is always greater than the setback."

-Brian Tracey

Rule #213:

"Once you change your mindset, you can attack everything."

-David Goggins

Rule #214:

"When life gets hard, You must go harder."

-Vinod Sharma

Rule #215:

"The wiser you are, the more worries you have; the more you know, the more it hurts."

-Ecclesiastes 1:18

Rule #216:

"Never try to be better than someone else. Always learn from others, never cease trying to be the best you can be that's under your control, and if you get too involved in the things you have no control over. It will adversely affect the things over which you have control."

-John Wooden

Rule #217:

"I DON'T LOSE, I WIN, I WIN. THAT'S MY JOB; THAT'S WHAT I DO."

-Keanu Reeves

(Devil's Advocate, 1997 film)

Rule #218:

"Be addicted to your passions, not your distractions."

-Anonymous

Rule #219:

"Stars can't shine without darkness."

-Frank Costello

Rule #220:

"The function of a man is to live, not to exist."

-Jack London

Rule #221:

"Life moves pretty quickly. If you don't stop and look around once in a while, you could miss it."

-Matthew Broderick

(Ferris Bueller's Day Off 1986 Film)

Rule #222:

"We may throw the dice, but the Lord determines how they fall".

-Proverbs 16:33

Rule #223:

"Become the man you want your son to be."

-Daniel G

Rule #224:

"If no one comes from the future to stop you from doing it, how bad of a decision can it be?"

-Michael Grassotti

Rule #225:

"You can't win in life if you are losing in your mind."

-Tony Gaskins Jr.

Rule #226:

"Sometimes you need to get hit in your head to realize you're in a fight."

-Michael Jordan

Rule #227:

"Life starts when you leave your comfort zone; you can't fly stuck in a cage."

-Anonymous

Rule #228:

"Don't judge your greatness by your shadow at sunset."

-Pythagoras

Rule #229:

"Trust gets you killed, love gets you hurt, and being real gets you hated."

-Johnny Cash

Rule #230:

"You have gotta want it as bad as you want to breathe."

-Tom Platz

Rule #231:

"Move with strategy, not with emotion."

-Deepak Bajaj

Rule #232:

"If the world hates you, just remember it hated me first."

-Jesus Christ

Rule #233:

"Fear is temporary; regret is permanent."

-Dan Skinner

Rule #234:

"The only place to go from failure is to win. You have to take it that far. Nobody wants to go that far because it's too scary. I have news for you: that's where winning is."

-Tom Platz

Rule #235:

"Nobody cares about you or your story until you win. So go win."

-Anonymous

Rule #236:

"For the moment, all discipline seems painful rather than pleasant, but later, it yields the peaceful fruit of righteousness to those who have been trained by it."

-Hebrews 12:11

Rule #237:

"Never let your loyalty keep you in situations your common sense would get you out of."

-Trent Shelton

Rule #238:

"When the wicked increase, transgression increases, but the righteous will look upon their downfall."

-Proverbs 29:16

Rule #239:

"When you rise, the people closest to you will offer more resistance."

-Adam Levine

Rule #240:

"Sometimes people hate you because of how other people love you."

-Karen Salmansohn

Rule #241:

"Whenever God wants to make a man powerful, he breaks him to pieces first."

-Charles H. Spurgeon

Rule #242:

“The best is yet to come, and won’t that be fine.”

-Frank Sinatra

Rule #243:

“Never forget the ones who helped you in difficult times, the ones who put you in difficult times, and the ones who left you in difficult times.”

-Gianni Grassotti

Rule #244:

“There’s no light without dark, no joy without pain, and no rainbow without a little rain.”

-Andrew Tate

Rule #245:

“How big would you dream if you knew you couldn’t fail?”

-Vincent Okeke

Rule #246:

“It only takes one bad day to make even the greatest hero a villain.”

-Joker

(Joker 2019 Film)

Rule #247:

“Excuses make today easy but tomorrow hard.”

-Rashmi

Rule #248:

“A great man is hard on himself, and a small man is hard on others.”

-Confucius

Rule #249:

“If speech is silver, then silence is gold.”

-Ibul Mubaarak

Rule #250:

“Love the hand that fate deals you, and play it as your own.”

-Marcus Aurelius

Rule #251:

“The most inspiring person is the one overcoming fear to do something, not the person who is excellent at it.”

-Ed Mylett

Rule #252:

"If I am killed, I die once, but to live in constant dread of it is to die over and over again."

-Abraham Lincoln

Rule #253:

"Vita incerta, mors certissima

(Life is uncertain; death is most certain)"

-Anonymous Latin quote

Rule #254:

"Everything we hear is an opinion, not a fact. Everything we see is perspective, not the truth."

-Marcus Aurelius

Rule #255:

"A real man puts in the work in the dark where it's only him and his thoughts."

-Eric Thomas

Rule #256:

"If you are ruled by the mind, you are a king; if by a body, a slave."

-Cato

Rule #257:

"Profits are better than wages."

-Jim Rohn

Rule #258:

"No mortal man is wise at all moments."

-Plany. The Elder

Rule #259:

"Learning is a gift even when pain is your teacher."

-James Garner

Rule #260:

"I prayed to God to protect me from my enemies. Suddenly, I began losing friends."

-Muhammad Ali

Rule #261:

"Maybe if we chased God as hard as we chase people, God would give us people we don't have to chase."

-Linda Kelechi

Rule #262:

"The master has failed more times than the beginner has even tried."

-Stephen McCraine

Rule #263:

"We will remember not our enemies' words, but our friends' silence."

-Anonymous

Rule #264:

"Never hate your enemies. It affects your judgment."

-Marlon Brando

(The Godfather 1972 Film)

Rule #265:

"Behind every successful fortune, there is a crime."

-Marlon Brando

(The Godfather 1972 Film)

Rule #266:

"Freedom will only come after you no longer trade your time for money."

-Andrew Tate

Rule #267:

"A friend to all is a friend to none."

-Aristotle

Rule #268:

"Rather fail with honor than succeed with fraud."

-Sophocles

Rule #269:

"If you cannot do the little things correctly, you will never be able to do the big things right."

-Admiral William H. McRaven

Rule #270:

"It is even better to act quickly than to hesitate until the time of action is past."

-Carl Von Clausewitz

Rule #271:

"Si vis pacem, para bellum"

(If you want peace, prepare for war)

-Anonymous (Latin Quote)

Rule #272:

"When a person can not control you, they will try to control how others view you."

-Gianni Grassotti

Rule #273:

"Never wish for what someone else has. Because you don't know what they did to get it, and you don't know what they are doing to keep it."

-Joey McIntyre

Rule #274:

"I am loyal because it is something instilled in me from a young age, not because I need that person."

-Gianni Grassotti

Rule #275:

"The moment when you want to quit is when you need to keep pushing."

-Anonymous

Rule #276:

"Don't let yourself get attached to anything you are not willing to walk out on in 30 seconds flat if you feel the heat around the corner."

-Robert Dinero

(Heat 1995 film)

Rule #277:

"Standing alone is for the strong. The weak hide in crowds"

-Anonymous

Rule #278:

"Airports see more sincere kisses than wedding halls. The walls of hospitals see more prayers than the walls of churches."

-Anonymous

Rule #279:

"Weak people take revenge. Strong people forgive. Intelligent people ignore."

-Albert Einstein

Rule #280:

"Today is difficult, tomorrow is much more difficult, but the day after tomorrow is beautiful. Most people die tomorrow evening."

-Jack Ma

Rule #281:

"To wake up every morning is a gift. To be able to accomplish what you want is a blessing."

-Gianni Grassotti

Rule #282:

"No tree can grow to heaven unless Its roots reach Hell."

-Carl Jung

Rule #283:

"The Realest people will make you uncomfortable at first, and the fakest people's job is talking and making people feel comfortable."

-Kanye West

Rule #284:

"Two things define you. Your patience when you have nothing and your attitude when you have everything."

-George Bernard

Rule #285:

"Never let anyone lower your goals. Others' expectations of you are determined by their limitations."

-Kwame Alexander

Rule #286:

"There's a huge difference between people who have good grades and smart people."

-Anonymous

Rule #287:

"Silence doesn't mean you ran out of things to say, only that you are trying not to say them."

-Kwame Alexander

Rule #288:

"Be careful of your words. They can be forgiven but never forgotten."

-Carl Sandburg

Rule #289:

"Contracts are like hearts; they are made to be broken."

-Michael Kenton

(Founder, 2016 film)

Rule #290:

"It takes one tree to make a thousand matches but one match to burn a thousand trees."

-Kelly Jones

Rule #291:

"In any fight, it's the guy who's willing to die that's going to win that inch."

-Al Pacino

(Any given Sunday, 1999 Film)

Rule #292:

"Real eyes realize real lies"

-Tupac Shakur

Rule #293:

"An idiot with a plan can beat a genius without one."

-Warren Buffett

Rule #294:

"Average goals will lead to an average life. You were not born just to be average."

-Anonymous

Rule #295:

"Space we can recover, time never"

-Napoleon Bonaparte

Rule #296:

"We judge others by their actions but judge ourselves by our intentions."

-Karen DiSanto

Rule #297:

"Looking towards mainstream media for the truth is like going to a brothel for love."

-Donald Trump Jr

Rule #298:

"To get over the past, you must first accept that it is over. No matter how often you revisit it, regret it, sweat it, it's over, and it can hurt you no more."

-Mandy Hale

Rule #299:

"All roads lead to you. Even the ones I took to forget you."

-Mahmoud Darwish

Rule #300:

"If you can't sleep at night, you are awake in someone else's dream."

-Anonymous Japanese legend

Rule #301:

"Not every man that is nice to you is flirting with you. Some mothers raised their children to be gentlemen."

-Michael B. Jordan

Rule #302:

"It takes six men to carry a guy to his grave; it only takes one woman to put him there."

-Howard Volkes

Rule #303:

"Life is one big head game, and you're losing."

-David Goggins

Rule #304:

"A man conquers the world by conquering himself."

-Zeno

Rule #305:

"There are so many people who have the ability and just refuse to get off that couch, go deeper, to go further. And that's where I gain the advantage."

-David Goggins

Rule #306:

"If you are the smartest person in the room, then you are in the wrong room."

-Confucius

Rule #307:

"No one cares what you did yesterday. It only matters what you do today."

-David Goggins

Rule #308:

"Confidence is built by facing what you fear."

-Neil Nasser

Rule #309:

"Why be normal when you can be the best?"

-Zlatan Ibrehemich

Rule #310:

"Dirty water doesn't stop plants from growing. So don't let negative words stop you from succeeding."

-Anonymous

Rule #311:

"I will not cause pain without allowing something new to be born."

-Isaiah 66:9

Rule #312:

"When boots were made of wood, men were made of steel."

-Charles Draper

Rule #313:

"Who is going to carry the boats?"

-David Goggins

Rule #314:

"There are two rules to success in life. One never reveal everything you know."

-Riddler

Rule #315:

"Not everybody wants to see you win. Succeed in silence."

-Pietro Grassotti

Rule #316:

"Discipline is the bridge between goals and accomplishments."

-Jim Rohn

Rule #317:

"A man who leaves in anger will always come back, but a man who left with a smile will not return."

-Idris Elba

Rule #318:

"Do not cross oceans for someone who would not even step in a puddle for you."

-Tony Robbins

Rule #319:

"A glow stick needs to be broken to glow."

-Anonymous

Rule #320:

"A fish with its mouth closed never gets caught."

-Tony Accardo

Rule #321:

"Show no mercy to those who have shown no loyalty."

-Neel N

Rule #322:

"To build confidence you have to take the leap even when the distance to the other side is unknown."

-Gianni Grassotti

Rule #323:

"Everything you want is on the other side of fear."

-Scarecrow

Rule #324:

"Average is the enemy, success is your responsibility, and change can occur instantly if you are willing to flip the switch."

-Bedros Keuilian

Rule #325:

"I was chasing perfection and excellence even though I would probably never catch it. But just because I was willing to chase something that is not guaranteed puts me ahead of my opponents who only chase certainties."

-Kobe Bryant

Rule #326:

"You're busy doubting yourself while others fear your true potential."

-Anonymous

Rule #327:

"If you are not prepared for the pain, you're never going to be something that matters."

-Andrew Tate

Rule #328:

“Life passes most people by when they make grand plans for it.”

-George Jung

Rule #329:

“You have two choices in life: suffer as a somebody or suffer as a nobody.”

-Andrew Tate

Rule #330:

“Hard work makes today hard but tomorrow easy.”

-Anonymous

Rule #331:

“I have no idea what I’m going to do tomorrow,

How exciting”

-Robin Williams (Mrs. Doubtfire 1993 Film)

Rule #332:

“Your body should be a tank, your mind should be a library, and your words should be philosophical.”

-Anonymous

Rule #333:

"Imagine playing Monopoly and never buying anything that could produce more money, just collecting $200 from go. That is how most people live their lives."

-Robert T. Kiyosaki

Rule #334:

"Train like you have never won; play like you have never lost."

-Lucas Lim

Rule #335:

"Stay humble. For those who flex fail to win the respect of others."

-Giuseppe Cerasuolo

Rule #336:

"Use the weekend to make the life you want, not to escape the one you have."

-Chervin Jefarieh

Rule #337:

"Money doesn't buy happiness; it buys crazy-ass happiness."

-Eminem

Rule #338:

"We ignore truths for temporary happiness."

-Nick Vujicic

Rule #339:

"Life and death are like light and dark. They're both always there. But people don't like to think about death, so subconsciously, they always look away from it."

-Yato

Rule #340:

"To look good in front of thousands, you need to outwork the thousands in front of no one."

-Damian Lillard

Rule #341:

"The temporary satisfaction of quitting is outweighed by the eternal suffering of being a nobody."

-Andrew Tate

Rule #342:

"Never argue with stupid people. They will drag you to their level and beat you with experience."

-Mark Twain

Rule #343:

"To be the better man, you must show them kindness even after they have stabbed you in the back."

-Pietro Cerasuolo

Rule #344:

"You do not need a lot of friends. Give me three absolute killers and we can take over the world."

-Joey Diaz

Rule #345:

"Although our intellect always longs for clarity and certainty, our nature often finds uncertainty fascinating."

-Carl Von Clausewitz

Rule #346:

"When you lose your money, you lose nothing. When you lose your health, you lose something. But when you lose your character, you lose everything."

-Anonymous

Rule #347:

"If you are a friend of everybody, you are an enemy to yourself."

-Mike Tyson

Rule #348:

"The only person you are destined to become is the person you choose to be."

-Ralph Waldo Emerson

Rule #349:

"To conquer the world, you have to conquer your mind, and to do that, you have to push yourself farther than you have ever been before."

-Gianni Grassotti

Rule #350:

"Focus on improving yourself, not proving yourself."

-Dan Martell

Rule #351:

"When nobody wakes you in the morning, and nobody waits for you at night, and when you can do whatever you want. What do you call it, freedom or loneliness?"

-Charles Bukowski

Rule #352:

"Remember, loving a girl more than yourself is a beautiful way of killing yourself."

-Anonymous

Rule #353:

"Your mind must be stronger than your feelings."

-Andrew Tate

Rule #354:

"Work hard in silence, let success be your noise."

-Frank Ocean

Rule #355:

"The best rewards come from the hardest battles."

-Andrew Tate

Rule #356:

"Metal takes longer to build, but it's stronger in the end."

-Anonymous

Rule #357:

"Inside a ring or out, nothing is wrong with going down. It's staying down that's the problem."

-Muhammad Ali

Rule #358:

"Dream so big that normal people think you are crazy."

-Anonymous

Rule #359:

"No one gives it to you; you must take it."

-Frank Costello

Rule #360:

"Work incredibly hard, and stay determined in pursuit of your goals. So much so that not even the devil would be happy to see you wake up each day."

-Robert Rylon

Rule #361:

"A man without a vision for his future Always returns to his past."

-Andrew Tate

Rule #362:

"Never lose yourself trying to hold onto somebody."

-Anonymous

Rule #363:

"The rules are simple: never lie to someone who trusts you. Never trust someone who lies to you."

-Andrew Tate

Rule #364:

"Women look for men with a future; Men look for women without a past."

-Oscar Wilde

Rule #365:

"In the end we only regret the chances we didn't take."

-John Gotti

Rule #366:

"A real man doesn't get jealous; He will just lose interest when he sees anyone can have your attention."

-Nat Lue

Rule #367:

"If you are the best-dressed man in the room, you are always the winner."

-Tristan (Talisman) Tate

Rule #368:

"We can easily forgive a child who is afraid of the dark. The real tragedy of life is when men are afraid of the light."

-John D. Rockefeller

Rule #369:

"I don't accept apologies. You did what made you happy at the expense of my emotions, and I understand it, but I won't accept it."

-Tristan (Talisman) Tate

Rule #370:

"When you destroy somebody's life with lies, take it as a loan. Because it will come back to you with interest."

-Anonymous

Rule #371:

"A strong man stands up for himself, and a stronger man stands up for others."

-Ben the Cow

Rule #372:

"Pain is inevitable, but suffering is optional."

-Buddha

Rule #373:

"You're always afraid to take the first step because all you see is every negative thing 10 miles down the road."

-Robin Williams

Rule #374:

"Life is like a book. Some chapters are happy, some sad, but all are necessary to get the whole story."

-Anonymous

Rule #375:

"The greatest victory is to conquer self."

-Plato

Rule #376:

"Life lessons will be repeated until they are learned."

-Dr. Marlo Archer

Rule #377:

"The power of thoughts can cause you either illness or recovery."

-Ibn Sina

Rule #378:

"Some things break you, and something makes you. But sometimes you need to be broken to be made."

-Kami Gracia

Rule #379:

"A man must recognize his emotions but he should never let them control him"

-Gianni Grassotti

Rule #380:

"People treat you exactly how they feel about you."

-Fran Seen

Rule #381:

"No one ever understands the inside because the only thing they can see is the outside."

-Yagmur

Rule #382:

"To succeed, one must be comfortable with the uncomfortable. Growth exists outside of your comfort zone."

-Sonia McDonald

Rule #383:

"The society that separates its scholars from its warriors will have its thinking done by cowards, and it's fighting by fools."

-Thucydides

Rule #384:

"It's your road and yours alone. Others may walk it with you, but no one can walk it for you."

-Rumi

Rule #385:

"Courage, above all things, is the first quality of a warrior."

-Carl Von Clausewitz

Rule #386:

"To measure the quality of your life, simply do nothing and see how it feels."

-Naval Ravikant

Rule #387:

"A pint of sweat saves a gallon of blood."

-George S. Patton

Rule #388:

"Champions do daily what everyone does occasionally."

-Kenny Smith

Rule #389:

"The struggle you're in today is developing the strength you need for tomorrow's success."

-Anonymous

Rule #390:

"We should not ask God for easier lives, but for the strength to endure a hard one."

-John F. Kennedy

Rule #391:

"In your weakest moments, the strongest version of you was waiting to be born. No pressure, no diamonds."

-Anonymous

Rule #392:

"Never let one mistake make you think you are a bad person."

-Salvatore (Sally Slices) Mandreucci

Rule #392:

"F-E-A-R has two meanings. Forget everything and run OR Face everything and rise."

-Zig Ziglar

Rule #394:

"Do not allow negative thoughts to enter your mind, for they are weeds that strangle confidence."

-Bruce Lee

Rule #395:

"One day, your life will flash before your eyes. Make sure it's worth watching."

-Gerard Way

Rule #396:

"The problem is people are being hated when they are real and are being loved when they are fake."

-Bob Marley

Rule #397:

"You're not going to score on every shot; it doesn't mean you shouldn't take the shots; it doesn't mean you shouldn't try to hit the goal."

-Jordan Peterson

Rule #398:

"Without a worthy opponent, a man cannot grow stronger."

-Mao Tse-Tung

Rule #399:

"If you give all your life to the earth, the earth will give you a tomb. But if you give all your life to Heaven, Heaven will give you a throne."

-St. Ephraim the Syrian

Rule #400:

"People bring up the past when intimidated by your present."

-Al Pacino

(Scarface 1983 Film)

Rule #401:

"Ego prevents you from learning from others. Envy prevents you from focusing on yourself. Anger prevents you from seeing clearly. Ignorance prevents you from making good decisions. Fear prevents you from seizing opportunities. Get rid of them all."

-David Negal

Rule #402:

"Through every night, there is a bright day after."

-Tupac Shakur

Rule #403:

"You don't know how fast time passes until you get there."

-Anonymous

Rule #404:

"Be your best self today. Everyone else is taken."

-Andrew Tate

Rule #405:

"You become very dangerous when you realize you can make it all alone."

-Arham Jain

Rule #406:

"One of the most fascinating things I learned about life is struggling is good."

-Joe Rogan

Rule #407:

"Love doesn't die in a day; respect does."

-Original Feral

Rule #408:

"If something is important enough, you should try. Even if the probable outcome is a failure."

-Elon Musk

Rule #409:

"Never trust words. Some people have sugar on their lips but venom in their hearts."

-Raja Sekhar Ummadi

Rule #410:

"Give a man a mask, and he will show his true self."

-Joker

(Joker 2019 Film)

Rule #411:

"I may think of you softly from time to time. But I'll cut off my hand before I ever reach for you again."

-Auther Miller

Rule #412:

"Only a fool learns from his mistakes. The wise man learns from the mistakes of others."

-Otto von Bismarck

Rule #413:

"A single lie is enough to create doubt in every truth."

-Arslan Zareef

Rule #414:

"It's hard to put a leash on a dog once you put a crown on its head."

-Tyrion Lannister

Rule #415:

"A world without loyalty is a world without trust."

-Gianni Grassotti

Rule #416:

"We can't change who we are; all we can do is just go with what we are."

-Rocky Balboa

(Rocky IV 1985 Film)

Rule #417:

"Never let someone who has not been in your shoes tell you how to lace them."

-Aaron Will

Rule #418:

"The happiness of your life depends on the quality of your thoughts."

-Marcus Aurelius

Rule #419:

"I hate a liar more than a thief. A thief is only after my salary; a liar is after my reality."

-50 Cent

Rule #420:

"Some people still discuss the old you because they can't access the new you."

-Fat Joe

Rule #421:

"Broken ribs don't hurt as bad as a broken heart."

-Trace M. Brown

Rule #422:

"We suffer more often in imagination than in reality."

-Lucius Seneca

Rule #423:

"Be grateful for the people in your life who tell you they care and show you they do."

-Steve Maraboli

Rule #424:

"Fiction is the lie through which we tell the truth."

-Albert Camus

Rule #425:

"Some people are not your friend; they are just scared to be your enemy."

-Anonymous

Rule #426:

"Men are like steel. When they lose their temper, they lose their worth."

-Chuck Norris

Rule #427:

"Don't be afraid to be alone. Sharks don't swim in packs but are still the most feared ocean predator."

-Anonymous

Rule #428:

"You can discover more about a person in an hour of play than a year of conversation."

-Plato

Rule #429:

"To live is to realize loss is a part of life. To make sure the only thing you don't lose is your faith in God, and you'll live forever."

-Gianni Grassotti

Rule #430:

"Trying to Define yourself is like trying to bite your teeth."

-Allan Watts

Rule #431:

"Go laugh in the places you cried. Win in the places you lost. Rewrite your story."

-Abhi Gupta

Rule #432:

"It's better to shoot for the moon and miss than shoot for the gutter and make it."

-Danny Trejo

Rule #433:

"They will never respect you if you keep giving them chances to disrespect you."

-Sangeetha Paramasivan

Rule #434:

"When trust is broken, sorry means nothing."

-Al Pacino

Rule #435:

"No man ever steps in the same river twice, for it is not the same river, and he is not the same man."

-Heraclitus

Rule #436:

"No man is free who is not a master of himself."

-Epictetus

Rule #437:

"Hard things are strengthening you for bigger things to come."

-Anonymous

Rule #438:

"No loss should be more regrettable to us than the loss of time, for it irretrievable."

-Zeno

Rule #439:

“Master your mind because a thought can ruin your day.”

-Calvin Nickson Jr.

Rule #440:

“Years of love have been forgotten in the hatred of a minute.”

-Edgar Allen Poe

Rule #441:

“Some people will judge you for changing; Others will celebrate you for growing. Choose your circle carefully.”

-Barb Schmidt

Rule #442:

“Impossible. A word to be found only in the dictionary of fools.”

-Napoleon Bonaparte

Rule #443:

“People hate on you when you can do things they can’t.”

-Anonymous

Rule #444:

“You don’t develop courage by being happy every day. You develop it by surviving difficult times and adversity.”

-Epicurus

Rule #445:

“There’s no one to impress. Live well for you. Improve for you. Most don’t get it.”

-Rich The Kid

Rule #446:

“The only true wisdom is in knowing you know nothing.”

-Socrates

Rule #447:

“The heaviest things in life are not iron and gold, But your unmade decisions.”

-Alex Hormozi

Rule #448:

“True friends are like stars; you can only recognize them when it's dark.”

-Bob Marley

Rule #449:

"The man who fails in the arena is more honorable than the one who never enters."

-Carl Saden

Rule #450:

"A person with something to prove will move mountains for you."

-Robert Greene

Rule #451:

"Self-respect comes from keeping the promises you made to yourself."

-Juan Acosta

Rule #452:

"When you pray for rain, you must deal with the mud too."

-Denzel Washington

(Remember the Titans 2000 Film)

Rule #453:

"Self-betrayal is putting someone else's feelings before your boundaries"

-Nat Lue

Rule #454:

"Your mind quits way before your body does."

-David Goggins

Rule #455:

"Actions prove who someone is; words just prove who they pretend to be."

-Anonymous

Rule #456:

"Raise your words, not your voice. It is rain that grows flowers, not thunder."

-Rumi

Rule #457:

"Accept people as they are, But place them where they belong."

-Ashley Elisé

Rule #458:

"Be aware of the quiet ones. They are the ones who think. The smarter you get, the less you speak."

-Keanu Reeves

Rule #459:

"Stay loyal, stay real, or stay away from me."

-Anonymous

Rule #460:

"The world suffers a lot. Not because of the violence of bad people. But from the silence of good people."

-Napoleon Bonaparte

Rule #461:

"Never regret the things you do wrong; regret the good things you did for the wrong person."

-Marc Chernoff

Rule #462:

"Be careful who you trust. People you know can hurt you the most."

-Ghost

(Call of Duty)

Rule #463:

"A good future needs some bad memories."

-Yash Shah

Rule #464:

"First, it hurts you, then it teaches you."

-Salvatore (Sally Slices) Madreucci

Rule #465:

"If you don't take risks, nothing will change."

-Anonymous

Rule #466:

"It's nice to be important, but it's important to be nice."

-Dwayne (The Rock) Johnson

Rule #467:

"The family you create as a man is more important than the family you come from."

-Shilpi Somaya Gowda

Rule #468:

"War is the continuation of Politics by other means."

-Carl Von Clausewitz

Rule #469:

"An uninformed majority will always lose the battle to an informed minority."

-Mirza Abdul Rahim

Rule #470:

"Those who are the hardest to love need it the most."

-Socrates

Rule #471:

"Don't expect to get what you give; not everyone has a heart like you."

-Falak Naag

Rule #472:

"Forgive others, not because they deserve forgiveness, But because you deserve peace."

-Johnathan Lockwood Huie

Rule #473:

"Once the rain is over, an umbrella becomes a burden to everyone. It is the same as how loyalty ends when benefits stop coming in."

-Anonymous

Rule #474:

"It is Better to act heartless than broken."

-Al Pacino

Rule #475:

"Never hide your bad side to make someone stay. Show your bad side and see who can stay."

-Gautami

Rule #476:

"A mistake repeated over and over again is not a mistake. It is a choice."

-Salvatore (Sally Slices) Madreucci

Rule #477:

"Your life becomes a masterpiece when you learn to master peace."

-Anonymous

Rule #478:

"A single death is a tragedy. A million deaths is a statistic."

-Joseph Stalin

Rule #479:

"Avoid people that act like victims of a problem they created."

-Anonymous

Rule #480:

"It is not heroes that make history, but history that makes heroes."

-Joseph Stalin

Rule #481:

"Have more than you show. Speak less than you know."

-William Shakespeare

Rule #482:

"They lose the day in expectation of the night and the night in fear of the dawn."

-Lucius Seneca

Rule #483:

"Never assume that loud is strong and quiet is weak."

-Cillian Murphy

Rule #484:

"The surest way to corrupt a youth is to instruct him to hold in higher esteem those who think alike than those who think differently."

-Nietzche

Rule #485:

"The more we value things outside of our control, the less control we have."

-Epictetus

Rule #486:

"Whoever is trying to bring you down is already below You."

-Salvatore (Sally Slices) Madreucci

Rule #487:

"In the matters of style, swim with the current. In the matters of principle stand like a rock."

-Thomas Jefferson

Rule #488:

"The best answer to anger is silence."

-Marcus Aurelius

Rule #489:

"Being too friendly invites much disrespect."

-Isohoboy

Rule #490:

"You sometimes think you want to disappear, but all you want is to be found."

-Kid Cudi

Rule #491:

"Even if you burn like fire, look like ice."

-Anonymous

Rule #492:

"A wise man accepts his pain, endures it, but does not add to it."

-Marcus Aurelius

Rule #493:

"I am not afraid of an army of lions led by a sheep; I am afraid of an army of sheep led by a lion"

-Alexander The Great

Rule #494:

"It's ok to lose to an opponent, but you must not lose to fear."

-Mr. Miyagi

(Karate Kid 1984 Film)

Rule #495:

"Every man dies, but not every man lives."

-William Wallace

Rule #496:

"They are all worried about where someone comes from. The only important thing is where someone is going."

-John Dillinger

(Public Enemy 2009 Film)

Rule #497:

"I'd rather be tired from work than be broke from laziness."

-Aaron Will

Rule #498:

"You have to train your mind to be stronger than your feelings, or else you will lose yourself."

-Mike Tyson

Rule #499:

"The person I needed the most taught me that I don't need anyone."

-Nitya Prakash

Rule #500:

"No man has the right to be an amateur in physical training. It is a shame for a man to grow old and not see the beauty and strength which his body is capable of."

-Socrates

Rule #501:

"Great men aren't born great. They grow to be great."

-Joseph Matteson

Rule #502:

"Bad friends ruin good morals."

-Bishop MarMarie Emmanuel

Rule #503:

"There are millions of pretty women, but few young successful men become the prize."

-Kevin Smith

Rule #504:

"Don't be a prisoner of your past. it was a lesson, not a life sentence."

-Salvatore (Sally Slices) Madreucci

Rule #505:

"To preserve liberty, it is essential that the whole body of people always possess arms."

-Henry Lee

Rule #506:

"Life is a party, and you are the piñata. It will continue to beat you until you break."

-Gianni Grassotti

Rule #507:

"A woman's beauty cannot manipulate a man who controls his urges. A man who cannot be manipulated is unconquerable."

-Johnathan Muncy Storm

Rule #508:

"Who you choose to be around you lets you know who you are."

-Sung Kang

Rule #509:

"Some people think to be strong is never to feel pain. In reality, the strongest people are those who feel, understand, and accept it."

-Charlotte Dawson

Rule #510:

"Nothing can affect a person's mind if they choose not to be affected by it."

-Caveman

Rule #511:

"Pain is your friend. Pain is your ally. Pain tells you when you have been wounded badly, But you know the best part about pain? It tells you that you are not dead yet."

-Anonymous Samurai

Rule #512:

"Be a master of the mind, not mastered by the mind."

-Zen proverb

Rule #513:

"Pay attention to what people say out of anger. They have been dying to tell you that."

-Anonymous

Rule #514:

"The sun is alone, too, but it still shines."

-Kanye West

Rule #515:

"Suffer now to live the rest of your life as a champion."

-Anonymous

Rule #516:

"Happiness can be found even in the darkest times but only when one remembers to turn on the light."

-Albus Dumbledore

(Harry Potter chamber of secrets 2002 film)

Rule #517:

"Missing out on temporary fun for permanent stability is never a loss."

-Issac Childress

Rule #518:

"The best time to plant a tree was 20 years ago; the second best time is now."

-Salvatore (Lucky) Luciano

Rule #519:

"Men can not discover new oceans unless they dare to lose sight of the shore."

-André Gide

Rule #520:

"Once we're thrown off our habitual paths, we think all is lost, but it's only here that the new and the good begins."

-Leo Tolstoy

Rule #521:

"A king may move a man, a father may claim a son, but that man can also move himself. Only then does that man's game truly begin."

-Edward Norton (Kingdom of Heaven 2005 Film)

Rule #522:

"Absence diminishes minor passions and inflames great ones, as wind douses a candle and fans a fire."

-La Rochefoucauld

Rule #523:

"Every son follows his father's example, not his advice."

-Charles F. Kettering\

Rule #524:

"Life is pure competition. Everything you want, someone else wants, too. That is why you must win. No matter what, stay winning."

-Breacher "Tim," KSK

Rule #525:

"A good son to his father is a good father to his son."

-Anonymous

Rule #526:

"When I have laid the bait for deer, I don't shoot at the first doe that comes to sniff but wait until the whole herd has gathered round."

-Otto Von Bismarck

Rule #527:

"It won't happen overnight, but if you quit, it won't happen at all."

-Grant Cardone

Rule #528:

"Everyone can be good at something. But not everyone can practice that something every day to try and perfect it; that separates winners from champions."

-Gianni Grassotti

Rule #529:

"You don't become confident by shouting affirmation in the mirror, but by a stack of undeniable proof that you are who you say you are"

-Alex Hormozi

Rule #530:

"A person who fails to fight for a better life is a person who has yet to go through the deepest parts of their life to know that they can endure any challenge."

-Gianni Grassotti

Rule #531:

"Until you realize your father was right, you will have a son who will always think you are wrong."

-Charles Wadsworth

Rule #532:

"No amount of money ever bought a second of time."

-Howard Stark

(Avengers Endgame, 2019 film)

Rule #533:

"As long as the majority is misinformed the minority will stay in power."

-Gianni Grassotti

Rule #534:

"Do the impossible, and you will never doubt yourself again."

-Andrew Tate

Rule #535:

"The Results you are looking for are in the work you are avoiding."

-Tory Eletto

Rule #536:

“Strong people suffer alone at night. Smile during the day, and tell their friends half and their parents nothing so they don’t worry about them.”

-Khabib Nurmagomedov

Rule #537:

“I don’t have dad's money; I have dad's work ethic.”

-Dale Litton

Rule #538:

“When you plan something well, there is no need to rush.”

-Thomas Shelby

(Peaky Blinders)

Rule #539:

“Life is peaceful when you limit your focus on others and aim your focus on yourself.”

-Gianni Grassotti

Rule #540:

"Worrying is like a rocking chair. It gives you something to do but gets you nowhere."

-Ryan Reynolds

(Van Wilder, 2002 Film)

Rule #541:

"If your path demands you to walk through hell, walk as if you own the place."

-Darynda Jones

Rule #542:

"The best way to fight the demons that chase you at night is to stop and turn around."

-Chaz Palminteri

Rule #543:

"It's not about what you are capable of; it is about what you are willing to do."

-Mike Tomlin

Rule #544:

"I accept failure as everybody excepts failure, but what I cannot accept is not trying."

-Michael Jordan

Rule #545:

"Everyone faces a point of isolation in life, it is what you chose to do during that time that separates you from the rest."

-Gianni Grassotti

Rule #546:

"Everybody has a chapter they don't read out loud."

-Joker

(Dark Knight 2008 Film)

Rule #547:

"If you fail at first. Remember that it takes six months to build a Rolls Royce and 13 hours to build a Toyota."

-Anonymous

Rule #548:

"People cry, not because they are sad but simply because they've been strong for too long."

-Johnny Depp

Rule #549:

"You can not rewrite your past, but you can grab a sheet of paper and write down your future."

-Himani Singh

Rule #550:

"I fear no man; if you breathe oxygen, it's a fair game."

-Conor McGregor

Rule #551:

"Never take criticism from a person you would not take advice from."

-Anonymous

Rule #552:

"How lucky am I to have something that makes saying goodbye so hard?"

-Winnie the poo

Rule #553:

"Sometimes it takes a painful experience to make us change our ways."

-Proverbs 20:30

Rule #554:

"You can't just keep blaming yourself. Just blame yourself once and move on."

-Homer Simpson

(Simpsons)

Rule #555:

"If it's meant to be, it will be. You won't have to force, convince, or worry over it. Let it flow, let it be, and let it come to you. You will attract everything you need."

-Anonymous

Rule #556:

"Accept your pain, but do not accept that you deserved it."

-Hoid

Rule #557:

"You want to die. Throw yourself in the sea, and you'll see yourself fighting to survive."

-Arabic Legend

Rule #558:

"The tragedy in a man's life is what dies inside him while he lives."

-Albert Schweitzer

Rule #559:

"Your friends should motivate and inspire you. Your circle should be well rounded and supportive, and keep it right, quality over quantity."

-Dulve Ruby

Rule #560:

"Death is nothing, but to live defeated and inglorious is to die daily."

-Napoleon Bonaparte

Rule #561:

"Believe in yourself and all that you are. Know that there is something inside you that is greater than any obstacle."

-Christian D. Larson

Rule #562:

"You can change what you do but can't change what you want."

-Thomas Shelby

Rule #563:

"Make sure your mirror is satisfied with you and your actions."

-Anonymous

Rule #564:

"God will only make you face challenges he knows you can overcome."

-Gianni Grassotti

Rule #565:

"Be who you are and say as you feel. Because those who matter don't mind, and those who do mind don't matter."

-Benard M. Baruch

Rule #566:

"It hurts when the person you'd take a bullet for is the one who pulls the trigger."

-Salvatore (Sally Slices) Madreucci

Rule #567:

"Move in silence. Only speak when it is time to say checkmate."

-Anonymous

Rule #568:

"You can not defeat me. I am prepared to die."

-Israel Adesanya

Rule #569:

"There's one thing a man should always do; it is never to let anyone change your point of view unless what they bring makes sense to you."

-Anonymous

Rule #570:

"I will die on my feet before I live on my knees."

-George Washington

Rule #571:

"Dreams without goals are just dreams."

-Denzel Washington

Rule #572:

"Be careful who you trust. Even salt and sugar look the same."

-Joker

(Joker 2019 Film)

Rule #573:

"A real loser is someone so afraid of losing they don't even try."

-Anonymous

Rule #574:

"I wish there were a way to know that you were in the good old days before you leave them."

-Andrew Bernard

Rule #575:

"Never run for a bus or a person because when one leaves, another always arrives."

-Bedanta Sarma

Rule #576:

"You must not fight too often with one enemy, or you will teach him all your art to war."

-Napoleon Bonaparte

Rule #577:

"A king needs a kingdom to be a king, not a queen."

-Anonymous

Rule #578:

"A ship is always safe at shore, but that is not what it is built for."

-Albert Einstein

Rule #579:

"The Game ends when the king falls, not when a pawn takes your queen."

-Andrew Tate

Rule #580:

"Somebody is in a hospital bed right now begging God for the opportunity you have. Don't you dare go to bed depressed? Count your blessings and shake it off."

-Paul Walker

Rule #581:

"If your absence does not affect them, then your presence never mattered."

-Anonymous

Rule #582:

"There is nothing wrong today, so enjoy the sunshine that comes through the car window while in traffic because you will have plenty of bad days to come."

-Andrew Tate

Rule #583:

"The same boiling water will make an egg hard and a potato soft, so you need to dictate your environment and not let the environment dictate you."

-Mike Stawski

Rule #584:

"Everybody that you fight is not your enemy, and everybody that helps you is not your friend."

-Mike Tyson

Rule #585:

"The speed of light is much faster than the speed of sound. Some people appear to be bright until you hear them talk."

-Alan Dundes

Rule #586:

"A man without enemies is a man without qualities."

-Max Culine

Rule #587:

"She wants to be with Superman but walks past Clark Kent daily."

-Anonymous

Rule #588:

"How can the sky be the limit when footprints are on the moon?"

-Paul Brandt

Rule #589:

"Never trust someone who has let you down more than twice. Once was a warning, the second time was a lesson; anything more than that is them taking advantage."

-Anonymous

Rule #590:

"Problems only exist in the human mind."

-Anthony de Mello

Rule #591:

"Keep people off balance and in the dark by never revealing the purpose behind your actions. If they have no clue what you are up to, they cannot prepare a defense."

-Robert Greene

Rule #592:

"Someone despises me. That is their problem."

-Marcus Aurelius

Rule #593:

"Never talk about your next step. Let your plans be as silent as the night."

-Gianni Grassotti

Rule #594:

"There is no tomorrow"

-Apollo Creed

(Rocky IV 1985 Film)

Rule #595:

"Accept yourself, love yourself, and keep moving forward. If you want to fly, you must eliminate what weighs you down."

-Roy T. Bennett

Rule #596:

"Change is inevitable, but growth is optional."

-Salvatore (Sally Slices) Madreucci

Rule #597:

"Success is not final. Failure is not fatal. It is the courage to continue that count."

-Winston Churchill

Rule #598:

"The best thing about being a man is building yourself into something worth bowing to."

-Andrew Tate

Rule #599:

"The days that break you are the days that make you."

-Anonymous

Rule #600:

"Even if a whole army surrounds me, I will not be afraid, even if enemies attack me. I will still trust God."

-Psalm 27:3

Rule #601:

"I asked for strength, and God gave me difficulties to make me strong; I asked for wisdom, and God gave me problems to solve; I asked for courage, and God gave me dangers to overcome; I asked for love, and God gave me troubled people to help. My prayers were answered."

-Anonymous

Rule #602:

"My flesh and my heart may fail, but God is the strength of my heart and my portion forever."

-Psalm 73:26

Rule #603:

"The devil only bothers those who do acts of good for each act is an insult to him and a praise to God."

-Gianni Grassotti

Rule #604:

"For those who draw the sword die by it."

-Jesus Christ

Rule #605:

"The same God that did not answer your prayers right away is the same God that did not punish you for your sins right away."

-Masidi Manjun

Rule #606:

"If you confess with your mouth that Jesus is Lord and believe in your heart that God raised him from the dead, you will be saved."

-Romans 10:9

Rule #607:

"Sadness that brings you closer to God is better than happiness that pulls you away from God."

-Anonymous

Rule #608:

"Good people pass away; the godly often die before their time. But no one seems to care or wonder why. No one seems to understand that God is protecting them from the evil to come. Those who follow godly paths will rest in peace when they die."

-Isaiah 57:1-2

Rule #609:

"Pain made me pray, but praying made me powerful"

-Tracy Cortez

Rule #610:

"I believe the more I study science, the more I believe in God."

-Sir Isaac Newton

Rule #611:

"Everyone could pray for my downfall but my faith is with God. God is my light, my strength, my father, and with God no one can stop me."

-Gianni Grassotti

Rule #612:

"Tears are prayers too; they travel to God when we cannot speak."

-Psalm 56:8

Rule #613:

"Hell can't be made attractive, so the devil made the road that leads them there attractive. Heaven is attractive, so God makes the road hard."

-Saint Basil the Great

Rule #614:

"The LORD makes firm the steps of the one who delights in him; though he may stumble, he will not fall, for the LORD upholds him with his hand."

-Psalm 37:23

Rule #615:

"When life is not a bed of roses, remember who wore the crown of thorns."

- Anonymous

Rule #616:

"I am not afraid of the thousands of enemies surrounding me on every side."

-Psalm 3:6

Rule #617:

"May God have mercy upon my enemies because I won't."

-General George S. Patton

Rule #618:

"But flee youthful lusts, and pursue righteousness, faith, love, peace with those who call on the Lord out of a pure heart and enjoy their companionship."

-2 Timothy 2:22

Rule #619:

"If a wall couldn't stop Joshua, the sea couldn't stop Moses, and death couldn't stop Jesus. Then, in Christ, nothing can stop you."

-Anonymous

Rule #620:

"Do not take revenge. Leave that for me."

-Romans 12:19

Rule #621:

"If you don't feel like praying, force it. Because something else also forces you not to pray."

-Dr. Bishop

Rule #622:

"But as for you, be strong and do not give up, for your work will be rewarded."

-2 Chronicles 15

Rule #623:

"A man's heart plans his way, but the Lord determines his steps."

-Proverbs 16:9

Rule #624:

"The righteous man falls seven times, and yet rises again."

-Proverbs 24:16

Rule #625:

"If God is the only person you have, then you have everything. Stop stressing over people."

-Anonymous

Rule #626:

"These people come near me with their mouths and honor me with their lips, but their hearts are far from mine. Their worship of me is based on merely human rules they have been taught."

-Isaiah 29:13

Rule #627:

"God has removed you from that table where you used to sit to save you from the host that was serving you poison."

-Anonymous

Rule #628:

"For I am not ashamed of the Gospel, because it is the power of God that brings salvation to everyone who believes"

-Romans 1:16

Rule #629:

"God will never give you everything you want, but he will always supply you with everything you need."

-Gianni Grassotti

Rule #630:

"The Lord laughs at the wicked, for he knows their day is coming."

-Psalms 37:13

Rule #631:

"When God wants to move you to bigger blessings, he'll allow a heavy thunderstorm to pour on you. Every plant grows after the rain."

-Jacqy Jack

Rule #632:

"The LORD is my light and my salvation; whom shall I fear? The LORD is the stronghold of my life; of whom shall I be afraid? When evil men advance against me to devour my flesh, enemies, and foes attack me, they will stumble and fall."

-Psalms 27:1

Rule #633:

"Sometimes the devil allows people to live a life free of trouble because he doesn't want them turning to God."

-Lenore Banks (God's Not Dead 2014 Film)

Rule #634:

"Though I walk through the valley of the shadow of death, I will fear no evil: for thou art with me; thy rod and thy staff comfort me."

-Psalm 23:4

Rule #635:

"You'll never come second by putting God first."

-Brian Houston

Rule #636:

"The righteous cry out, and the LORD hears them; he delivers them from all their troubles."

-Psalm 34:17-18

Rule #637:

"I asked God for Water, and he gave me the ocean. I asked God for light, and he gave me the sun. I asked God for an angel, and he gave me my mother."

-Anonymous

Rule #638:

"What matter of this man is this, that even the winds and sea obey him?"

-Matthew 8:27

Rule #639:

"When the devil keeps asking you to look into the past, there's something in the future he doesn't want you to see."

-Anonymous

Rule #640:

"The same power that raised Christ from the dead is living in you."

-Romans 8:11

Rule #641:

"God will put you back together before the people that broke you."

-Anonymous

Rule #642:

"For if you place your problems in front of God, there is no more for you to do. Do not overthink it because if it is in God's hands, it will happen, and nothing will stop it. If not, then God has a better plan for you."

-Gianni Grassotti

Rule #643:

"Be so confident in God's plan that you don't get upset when things don't go your way."

-Claudine Joseph

Rule #644:

"I lift my eyes to the mountains. Where does my help come from? My help comes from the Lord, the Maker of heaven and earth."

-Psalm 121:1-2

Rule #645:

"If you don't stand firm in your faith, you won't stand at all."

-Isaiah 7:9

Rule #646:

"The giant in front of you is never bigger than the God inside you."

-1John 4:4

Rule #647:

"God is our light and our answers. Those who stay in the dark are foolish for they will not be able to see what they are missing."

-Gianni Grassotti

Rule #648:

"For the lord, your God is the one who goes with you to fight for you against your enemies to give you victory."

-Deuteronomy 20:4

Rule #649:

"God gave you gifts most would die for."

-Anonymous

Rule #650:

"Do you not know that your body is a temple of the Holy Spirit, who is in you, whom you have received from God?"

-1 Corinthians 6:19-20

Rule #651:

"For the Lord our God is with you wherever you go."

-Joshua 1:9

Rule #652:

"I took the tests that God gave me and made them testaments of what I stand for today."

-Gianni Grassotti

Rule #653:

"The person who gets to heaven is not the sinless person. The sinner repented and placed their faith in Jesus Christ."

-Anonymous

Rule #654:

"A true man prays for a person who is struggling and doesn't just tell others how bad they feel about that person's struggles."

-Gianni Grassotti

Rule #655:

"The devil wouldn't be attacking you so hard if something wasn't valuable inside you."

-Matthew McConaughey

Rule #656:

"If God is on our side, who can stand against us?"

-Romans 8:31

Rule #657:

"I believe in God because I know no matter how hard I try, I can never be the perfect father for my children, but I know that God will."

-Anonymous

Rule #658:

"Every moment, good and bad, is part of my plan for you."

-Ephesians 1:11

Rule #659:

"A man who blames God for not answering his prayers immediately needs to thank God for not punishing him for his sins immediately."

-Anonymous

Rule #660:

"To experience God's true might, you must be able to trust God even when your whole world is turned upside down."

-Gianni Grassotti

Rule #661:

"The only easy day was yesterday."

-United States Navy Seals

——---

"It's not the backstab that kills you. It's when you turn around to see who did it."

-Kendrick Perkins

Rule #662:

"And do not fear those who kill the body but cannot kill the soul; rather fear him who can destroy both soul and body in hell."

-Matthew 10:28

Rule #663:

"The pain means you are alive; the scars mean you survived."

-Anonymous

Rule #664:

"As a dog returns to its vomit, a fool will return to sin."

-Proverbs 26:11

Rule #665:

"Death smiles at us all. All a man can do is smile back."

-Marcus Aurelius

Rule #666:

"Vivo Christo Rey"

(Long live Christ the King)

-Jose Sánchez

Rule #667:

"The devil can offer you the most beautiful things. To have the pleasure of seeing you lose everything."

-Anonymous

Rule #668:

"No weapon that is used against you shall defeat you."

-Isaiah 54:17

Rule #669:

"If you don't exceed your limits by overcoming your fears, then your fears will become your limits."

-John Beckmann

Rule #670:

"God will grant you any gift you ask, but it will always come as a reward from hard labor."

-Leonardo Di Vinci

Rule #671:

"Be comfortable waiting a little longer for the things you deserve."

-Abdi Hassan

Rule #672:

"Those who come to seek the mercy of God's will are no strangers."

-Moses

Rule #673:

"A blade does not become strong until it goes through the fire."

-Anonymous

Rule #674:

"The Lord is near. Do not be anxious about anything, but in everything, by prayer and petition, with thanksgiving, present your requests to God."

-Philippians 4:4

Rule #675:

"It is in the dark where you find the strongest version of yourself."

-Arlene Ambrose

Rule #676:

"God never gives you a dream that matches your budget. He's not checking your bank account; he is checking your faith."

-Mark Wahlberg

Rule #677:

"Some doors are still locked because you are not ready yet for what's waiting on you in the next room."

-Christopher Pike

Rule #678:

"I will be a father to you, and you shall be sons and daughters to me, says the lord almighty."

-2 Corinthians 6:18

Rule #679:

"A man who conquers himself is greater than a man who conquers a thousand men in battle."

-Buddha

Rule #680:

"For with God, nothing is impossible."

-Luke 1:37

Rule #681:

"I know a boss in a Honda and a bum in a Benz. Never let possessions fool you."

-Morgan Rainey

Rule #682:

"You are my battle-ax and sword," says the LORD. "With you, I will shatter nations and destroy many kingdoms."

-Jeremiah 51:20

Rule #683:

"To be a beast, you must be able to walk through hell and be grateful that your legs are working."

-Anonymous

Rule #684:

"People ruin their lives by their foolishness and then are angry at the Lord."

-Proverbs 19:3

Rule #685:

"If they are true to you, they will teach you the game, not try to play you in it."

-Anonymous

Rule #686:

"Whoever is not with me is against me, and whoever does not gather with me scatters."

-Luke 11:23

Rule #687:

"Learn to be quiet. Everyone is not on your team; they want to know the game plan."

-Margie Richer

Rule #688:

"I trained while you talked,

I practiced while you partied,

I pursued while you pushed it aside,

I prayed while you sinned.

The bottom line is I worked while you watched, so don't say it must be nice when you could have the same thing."

-Gianni Grassotti

Rule #689:

"Hurting someone's feelings is as easy as throwing a rock in the ocean, but you never know how deep that rock goes."

-Anonymous Arabic Legend

Rule #690:

"When life is heavy and hard to take, go off yourself. Enter the silence. Bow in prayer. Don't ask questions: Wait for hope to appear. Don't run from trouble. Take it full face. The "worst" is never the worst."

-Lamentations 3:28-30

Rule #691:

"To survive life's greatest challenges a person must have the body of an athlete, the mind of a stoic, and the spirit of a warrior."

-Gianni Grassotti

Rule #692:

"He loves you so much. God has bought you with a price. He has given his life to save and give you a new life. God, help us to glorify you with our bodies."

-1 Corinthians 6:19-20

Rule #693:

"Warriors are not what you think of as warriors. The warrior is not someone who fights, for no one has the right to take another life. The warrior for us is the one who sacrifices himself for the good of others."

-Sitting Bull

Rule #694:

"The pain you've been feeling can't compare to the joy coming."

-Romans 8:18

Rule #695:

“Build as it will never end. But prepare like it will end tomorrow.”

-Anonymous

Rule #696:

“Trust in the LORD with all your heart and lean not on your understanding; in all your ways acknowledge him, and he will make your paths straight.”

-Proverbs 3:5-6

Rule #697:

“True measure of a man is not what he can show to the world, but what he hides from it.”

-Gianni Grassotti

Rule #698:

“Eagles don’t hunt flies.”

-Frank Costello

Rule #699:

“It takes nothing to join the crowd; it takes everything to stand alone.”

-Hans F. Hasen

Rule #700:

"There is no better feeling in the world than waking up to see another day and realize that life is what you make of it."

-Gianni Grassotti

Rule #701:

"Never let your brother stand alone in bad times."

-Anonymous

Rule #702:

"They call me a dreamer, yet I am the one who is losing sleep trying to make it happen."

-Gianni Grassotti

Rule #703:

"Nothing is worse than seeing your friend go down the wrong path."

-Anonymous

Rule #704:

"Greatness is not guarding yourself against the people; greatness is being accepted by the people."

-Mike Tyson

Rule #705:

"Silence is the best reply to a fool."

-Imam Ali

Rule #706:

"What we do in life ripples in eternity."

-Marcus Aurelius

Rule #707:

"They act as if they wish me well, so I act as if I believe them."

-Anonymous

Rule #708:

"A woman that can be bought isn't worth having."

-Kingpin

Rule #709:

"When you choose peace, it comes with many goodbyes."

-Anonymous

Rule #710:

"Don't worry about the people that God removed from your life. Because he saw things you didn't see, heard things you didn't hear, and made moves you wouldn't make."

-Steve Harvey

Rule #711:

"The version of me you created in your mind is not my responsibility."

-Alisha K

Rule #712:

"You must put in the effort to get the life you want."

-Andrew Tate

Rule #713:

"The only way some people will learn to appreciate you is by losing you."

-Pankaj Yaduvanshi

Rule #714:

"With God, Everything is possible; you just have to trust it."

-Tristan (Talisman) Tate

Rule #715:

"People that know their purpose in life do not waste their time being pushed around."

-Gianni Grassotti

Rule #716:

"Never worry about what the other guy is doing. That is a waste of energy."

-Iman Gadzhi

Rule #717:

"Once the pain becomes a habit, success becomes a lifestyle."

-Anonymous

Rule #718:

"We all love ourselves more than other people but care more about other people's opinions than our own."

-Marcus Aurelius

Rule #719:

"Losers quit once they fail. Winners will fail until they win."

-Gianni Grassotti

Rule #720:

"A man can make ten friends in one year, but it takes ten years to make one brother."

-Gianni Grassotti

Rule #721:

"You can chase the life you want or settle with the life you got."

-Gianni Grassotti

Rule #722:

"The axe forgets; the tree remembers."

-African Proverb

Rule #723:

"If they believe the lies without hearing your side of the story, they are already looking for a way to be against you."

-Anonymous

Rule #724:

"If speed kills me, don't cry because I was smiling."

-Paul Walker

Rule #725:

"Life is a series of risks and unless you are willing to take that first leap you will remain in the same spot".

-Gianni Grassotti

Rule #726:

"It requires more courage to suffer than to die."

-Napoleon Bonaparte

Rule #727:

"A smooth sea never made a skilled sailor."

-Franklyn D. Roosevelt

Rule #728:

"Regrets, I've had a few. But then again, there are too few to mention."

-Frank Sinatra

Rule #729:

"Men hate betrayal more than they love sex."

-Anonymous

Rule #730:

"When it is grim, be the grim reaper."

-Andy Reid

Rule #731:

"I Shall either find a way or make one."

-Hannibal

Rule #732:

"Love me or hate me, you watched, and that is all you could do."

-Pete Weber

Rule #733:

"Focus on making money instead of getting good grades."

-Anonymous

Rule #734:

"There is no such thing as accident; it is fate misnamed."

-Napoleon Bonaparte

Rule #735:

"Sometimes healing and growth looks a lot like failures and mistakes."

-Stephen Castro

Rule #736:

"That's life."

-Frank Sinatra

Rule #737:

"It is better to be hated for what you are than to be loved for what you are not."

-Andre Gide

Rule #738:

"It will hurt for a while; it will not be today, tomorrow, or next week, but eventually, it will get better."

-Dana Grassotti

Rule #739:

"Work so hard you no longer call it a dream; You call it life."

-Anonymous

Rule #740:

"You are only as strong physically as you are mentally."

-Isabella Ronacher

Rule #741:

"The calmer you are, the clearer you think."

-Keith Knox

Rule #742:

"With a nice suit and a smile, anything in life can be yours."

-Gianni Grassotti

Rule #743:

"If you get into business to solve problems, you'll make money. If you get into business to make money, you'll have problems."

-Alan Stern

Rule #744:

"Don't always trust somebody when they say they want the best for you because even the devil offers people everything they want."

-Nicholas Ambrosino

Rule #745:

"You won't win because I won't lose."

-Anonymous

Rule #746:

"For a person to be able to live in the moment is momentous in itself. For tomorrow is uncertain just as the rest of our future."

-Gianni Grassotti

Rule #747:

"I did it alone. I did it tired. I did it broke, and I did it scared. I know I'll survive."

-Anonymous

Rule #748:

"The tears you shed from losing someone you love is the water used to make you grow stronger."

-Gianni Grassotti

Rule #749:

"If a man knows not to which port he sails. Then no wind is favorable."

-Lucius Seneca

Rule #750:

"Most are not proud of you. They are just surprised that you keep on making things happen."

-Gianni Grassotti

Rule #751:

"Your younger self had a dream. Don't let that little guy down."

-Anonymous

Rule #752:

"Life starts to make sense when strangers clap louder for you than people you thought cared about you."

-Gianni Grassotti

Rule #753:

"Two emotions will control people's lives. Fear and greed."

-Robert T. Kiyosaki

Rule #754:

"I have more respect for people who openly say they don't like me, more than people who pretend to like me."

-Gianni Grassotti

Rule #755:

“Do exactly what they said you couldn’t do. You made yourself a promise. Don’t you dare break it?”

-Anonymous

Rule #756:

“My mom taught me to love unconditionally, and my father taught me who to love.”

-Gianni Grassotti

Rule #757:

“Nothing is more dangerous than a man who healed his wounds alone. Because that man has had more conversations with his mind than he has ever had with any human.”

-Tom Hardy

Rule #758:

“Without pain, defeat, suffering, and heartbreak, a man cannot reach his full potential. Because it is these key elements that will push a man to become the greatest version of himself.”

-Gianni Grassotti

Rule #759:

"Sometimes, when you are in a dark place, you think you have been buried. You have been planted."

-Christine Caine

Rule #760:

"For a boy to truly become a man, he has to train like Rocky, fight like Mike Tyson, think like Einstein, speak like Aristotle, and be cunning like James Bond."

-Gianni Grassotti

Rule #761:

"If you lost them but found peace, you won."

-Anonymous

Rule #762:

"If you are not going to do it for yourself, then do it for your parents and grandparents who sacrificed everything just to get you to where you are today."

-Gianni Grassotti

Rule #763:

"A man who sacrifices his goals for a woman winds up losing both."

-Andrew Tate

Rule #764:

"You sit at the kid's table discussing what games to play. I sit at the king's table discussing how to win the game."

-Gianni Grassotti

Rule #765:

"Those who say it can not be done should not interrupt those in the middle of doing it."

-George Bernard Shaw

Rule #766:

"A person should only give their umbrella to the person who stood in the rain with them when they have the opportunity to be dry."

-Gianni Grassotti

Rule #767:

"A son does not judge his father, but he remembers every moment his father judged him."

-John Green

Rule #768:

"The love that a boy has for their mother can never be described by words, for there is no length a boy would not go to just to see his mother smile."

-Gianni Grassotti

Rule #769:

"When you became a man, you put away the childish things."

-1Corinthians 13:11

Rule #770:

"Real men despise battle but never run from it."

-George Washington

Rule #771:

"The trouble with fiction is that it makes too much sense, whereas reality never makes sense."

-Aldous Huxley

Rule #772:

"Whenever you face the enemy, take them head-on. The man who sits for cover meets their unwelcomed fate."

-Richard Di Santo

(United States Army, 9th Infantry Squad leader, Vietnam War)

Rule #773:

"Worrying doesn't take away tomorrow's troubles; it takes away today's peace."

-Judson Brewer

Rule #774:

"Put things in the past and look forward to the future."

-Karen DiSanto

Rule #775:

"Always keep going, no matter what happens"

-Kobe Bryant

Rule #776:

"Never stress over the little things and let life play out."

-Karen DiSanto

Rule #777:

"Quotes don't work unless you do."

-Anonymous

9 789363 301122

Printed by Libri Plureos GmbH in Hamburg,
Germany